Greater Than a Tourist Book Series

I think the series is wonderful and beneficial for tourists to get information before visiting the city.
-Seckin Zumbul, Izmir Turkey

I am a world traveler who has read many trip guides but this one really made a difference for me. I would call it a heartfelt creation of a local guide expert instead of just a guide.
-Susy, Isla Holbox, Mexico

New to the area like me, this is a must have!
-Joe, Bloomington, USA

This is a good series that gets down to it when looking for things to do at your destination without having to read a novel for just a few ideas.
-Rachel, Monterey, USA

Good information to have to plan my trip to this destination.
-Pennie Farrell, Mexico

Aptly titled, you won't just be a tourist after reading this book. You'll be greater than a tourist!
-Alan Warner, Grand Rapids, USA

Thank you for a fantastic book.
-Don, Philadelphia, USA

Chrissie Stephen

Great ideas for a port day.
-Mary Martin USA

Even though I only have three days to spend in San Miguel in an upcoming visit, I will use the author's suggestions to guide some of my time there. An easy read - with chapters named to guide me in directions I want to go.
-Robert Catapano, USA

Great insights from a local perspective! Useful information and a very good value!
-Sarah, USA

This series provides an in-depth experience through the eyes of a local. Reading these series will help you to travel the city in with confidence and it'll make your journey a unique one.
-Andrew Teoh, Ipoh, Malaysia

Tourists can get an amazing "insider scoop" about a lot of places from all over the world. While reading, you can feel how much love the writer put in it.
-Vanja Živković, Sremski Karlovci, Serbia

>TOURIST

GREATER THAN A TOURIST – SOUTHAMPTON & THE NEW FOREST UNITED KINGDOM

50 Travel Tips from a Local

Chrissie Stephen

Chrissie Stephen

Greater Than a Tourist- Southampton & The New Forest United Kingdom Copyright © 2018 by CZYK Publishing LLC. All Rights Reserved.

All rights reserved. No part of this book may be reproduced in any form or by any electronic or mechanical means including information storage and retrieval systems, without permission in writing from the author. The only exception is by a reviewer, who may quote short excerpts in a review.

Cover designed by Ivana Stamenković
Cover images: https://pixabay.com/en/southampton-night-shots-england-2293032/
https://pixabay.com/en/storm-clouds-sky-weather-thunder-2187000/

Greater Than a Tourist
Visit our website at www.GreaterThanaTourist.com

Lock Haven, PA
All rights reserved.

ISBN: 9781980560104

>TOURIST
50 TRAVEL TIPS FROM A LOCAL

Chrissie Stephen

BOOK DESCRIPTION

Are you excited about planning your next trip?
Do you want to try something new?
Would you like some guidance from a local?

If you answered yes to any of these questions, then this Greater Than a Tourist book is for you.

Greater Than a Tourist- Southampton & The New Forest United Kingdom by Chrissie Stephen offers the inside scoop on Southampton & The New Forest. Most travel books tell you how to travel like a tourist. Although there is nothing wrong with that, as part of the Greater Than a Tourist series, this book will give you travel tips from someone who has lived at your next travel destination.

In these pages, you will discover advice that will help you throughout your stay. This book will not tell you exact addresses or store hours but instead will give you excitement and knowledge from a local that you may not find in other smaller print travel books.

Travel like a local. Slow down, stay in one place, and get to know the people and the culture. By the time you finish this book, you will be eager and prepared to travel to your next destination.

Chrissie Stephen

>TOURIST

TABLE OF CONTENTS

BOOK DESCRIPTION
TABLE OF CONTENTS
DEDICATION
ABOUT THE AUTHOR
HOW TO USE THIS BOOK
FROM THE PUBLISHER
OUR STORY
WELCOME TO
> TOURIST
INTRODUCTION
1. The Tale of Three Rivers
2. Museums to Visit in Southampton
The SeaCity Museum
Solent Sky Museum
3. For Art Lovers...
4. Good Beer and History Combined…
5. Across The Dark Water
6. A History of Cruise Ships
7. A Very Special Cruise Ship
8. Container Ships & Cargo
9. Famous People from Southampton & Waterside
10. Serious Retail Therapy!
11. Eling Tide Mill
12. Hythe, With the Oldest Pier Railway
13. Dibden & Dibden Purlieu
14. Fawley & the Oil Refinery

Chrissie Stephen

15. Calshot - With Such a Rich History
16. The Flying Boats
17. Calshot for Speed!
18. Pretty Coloured Beach Huts
19. The Isle of Wight
20. Great Sailing...And A Good Rowing Challenge...
21. A Royal Favourite
22. Dinosaur Island!
23. The Importance of the Needles
24. Isle of Wight Crab Cakes
25. The Beautiful New Forest
26. A Rich History
27. Ponies Galore!
29. Pannage
31. Beaulieu
32. Palace House
33. Beaulieu Abbey
34. A Passion for Cars...
35. And for Chocolates!
36. Hatchet Pond
37. Bucklers Hard
38. The Jewel of the New Forest
39. Lepe Country Park
40. Oysters by the Ton!
41. Lymington
42. The Story of the Golden Post Box
43. Rhinefield – a Great Ornamental Drive
44. Brockenhurst
45. New Forest Wildlife Park

46. Lyndhurst
47. Romsey
48. Lord Mountbatten
49. The City of the Statues
50. Knights and Bollards!
TOP REASONS TO BOOK THIS TRIP
> TOURIST
GREATER THAN A TOURIST
> TOURIST
GREATER THAN A TOURIST
NOTES

>TOURIST

DEDICATION

This book is dedicated to my three children and the fun times we had in the area.

Chrissie Stephen

ABOUT THE AUTHOR

For a number of years, Chrissie Stephen and her young family lived on the edge of the New Forest. Exploring the area, she found there was so much to see and do and soon discovered the rich history of the area.

With so many happy memories of time spent at Buckler's Hard, helping out with a large Easter bunny order at the chocolate shop in Beaulieu and the popular Auto Jumbles organised by Lord Montagu, Chrissie firmly believes that the area is perfect for all the family. Her elder daughter enjoyed watching the ponies, her son crab fishing at Eling Wharf, whilst her younger daughter was baptised in Beaulieu Abbey. Happy memories...

Chrissie Stephen

HOW TO USE THIS BOOK

The Greater Than a Tourist book series was written by someone who has lived in an area for over three months. The goal of this book is to help travelers either dream or experience different locations by providing opinions from a local. The author has made suggestions based on their own experiences. Please do your own research before traveling to the area in case the suggested places are unavailable.

Chrissie Stephen

FROM THE PUBLISHER

Traveling can be one of the most important parts of a person's life. The anticipation and memories that you have are some of the best. As a publisher of the Greater Than a Tourist book series, as well as the popular 50 Things to Know book series, we strive to help you learn about new places, spark your imagination, and inspire you. Wherever you are and whatever you do I wish you safe, fun, and inspiring travel.

Lisa Rusczyk Ed. D.
CZYK Publishing

Chrissie Stephen

OUR STORY

Traveling is a passion of the "Greater than a Tourist" series creator. Lisa studied abroad in college, and for their honeymoon Lisa and her husband toured Europe. During her travels to Malta, an older man tried to give her some advice based on his own experience living on the island since he was a young boy. She was not sure if she should talk to the stranger but was interested in his advice. When traveling to some places she was wary to talk to locals because she was afraid that they weren't being genuine. Through her travels, Lisa learned how much locals had to share with tourists. Lisa created the "Greater Than a Tourist" book series to help connect people with locals. A topic that locals are very passionate about sharing.

Chrissie Stephen

WELCOME TO
> TOURIST

Chrissie Stephen

INTRODUCTION

The sea once it casts its spell, holds one in its net of wonder forever...
Jacques Cousteau.

Southampton is an attractive port city that is situated on the south coast of England. The city lies at the northernmost point of Southampton Water at the confluence of the Rivers Test and Itchen. A third river, the Hamble, flows into Southampton Water just a little further south.

Excavations have revealed that there has been a settlement in the area since the Stone Age. Later in Roman times, it became a defensive settlement named Clausentum and was established as a trading port.

During the Anglo Saxon period, the settlement grew in size and became known first as Hamtun and later as Hampton and these names gave both the city and the county their names.

Today, it is the largest University City in Hampshire and lies 75 miles (121km) southwest of London and 19 miles (31 km) west of Portsmouth. Its name is often abbreviated to So'ton or Soton and its residents are Sotonian. Southampton has a popular football team – 'The Saints'.

It is one of the busiest ports in the UK welcoming thousands of cruise passengers each year, many of them having just a few hours to enjoy Southampton, the Waterside and the beautiful New Forest...

Chrissie Stephen

>TOURIST

1. The Tale of Three Rivers

Southampton is situated on the confluence of two rivers – the Test and the Itchen where they flow into Southampton Water - the tidal estuary that flows into the Solent. The rivers flow into Southampton Water at its most northwesterly point and the Hamble joins Southampton Water just a little further south. The area has a rich heritage in boat building and yachting.

The River Test is 40 miles (64 km) in length and its source is near Ashe. It is a lovely river that has cut through chalk so its waters are crystal clear and the river is well known for good trout fishing Watercress grows in abundance along its tributaries. The River Test and the surrounding countryside feature in the popular children's story Watership Down by Richard Adams.

The Itchen rises in mid-Hampshire and flows for 28 miles (45 km) before joining Southampton Water just below Itchen Bridge. It is a river that is popular for fly fishing and also has areas for growing watercress. It is an important river as it is home to a number of protected species including brown trout, water voles and white-clawed crayfish.

The source of the Hamble is in Bishop's Waltham and the river is just 7.5 miles (12 km) in length. The river joins Southampton Water near Hamble-Le- Rice and is tidal for half of its length. In the 14th century it was a major ship building centre and was more important than Portsmouth. Today it is popular for sailing and has three busy marinas.

2. Museums to Visit in Southampton

To many, the city's distinctive medieval Bargate is an emblem of Southampton. Constructed in 1180, with further alterations in 1290, the Bargate used to be the main entrance to the town and was a part of the defensive walls. Today it is a grade 1 listed building and work began in November 2018 on transforming the area near the Bargate by demolishing the old and unused shopping centre and building a broad terraced garden street linking the Bargate with Queensway.

The garden street will mimic the gardens that used to run along the city wall, with shops and open air coffee shops, private accommodation. Remaining parts of the old city wall will be highlighted by spotlights. The project will be completed in autumn 2019.

The SeaCity Museum

This popular museum is housed in Southampton's old magistrates' court and police station, and was opened on 10 April 2012 to mark the centenary of RMS Titanic's departure from the city. The museum traces Southampton's rich maritime as the 'gateway to the world' and has a display showing how the Titanic disaster impacted Southampton.

>TOURIST

Solent Sky Museum

Situated in the city, this museum follows the history of aviation in the city, Solent and Hampshire. It looks at The Supermarine Aircraft Company based in Southampton and its S6 and Supermarine Spitfire, as well as the flying boats that were once based at Calshot.

3. For Art Lovers...

Situated near to the SeaCity Museum in the Civic Centre, is the Southampton City Art Gallery. It is considered by many to be the finest collection of art in Southern England and has more than 5,300 pieces on display. Opened in 1939, the museum has an interesting collection of works that trace the Renaissance through six centuries with 3,500 works including those by Dutch, French and Italian artists.

The main focus for the museum however, is British 20th century and contemporary art and the museum has a number of important works. The collection of paintings continues to grow as the museum often receives donations or bequests.

There are regular exhibitions held in the museum including sculpture, painting, drawing, photography and film works.

Chrissie Stephen

4. Good Beer and History Combined...

The Wool House is a beautiful medieval warehouse that was built by Cistercian monks in the late 14th century, close to the Roman city walls. The warehouse was used for storing wool that was processed in Romsey and going to be exported to Venice and Genoa.

The warehouse was not used for many years but in the 19th century, during Napoleonic times it was used to house French prisoners of war and their names can still be seen carved into the wooden roof beams. For many years, the building was used to house the city's maritime museum which was relocated to SeaCity in 2011.

Since then the Wool House has been the Dancing Man Micro Brewery and serves its own range of craft beers that are brewed on the premises and offers visitors great views over the waterfront whilst enjoying great beer!

5. Across The Dark Water

This is the title of a play written by Ben Musgrave and Neil Duffield that was performed at historical sites in Southampton throughout 2015 as part of the commemoration of the 600th anniversary of the Battle of Agincourt.

Although most people think of the battle as a great victory for Henry V, the 'War King' and it has been immortalised by Shakespeare and others, 'Across the Dark Water' tells how history could have been very different.

The play is set in 1415 and tells how troops were mustering just outside the fortified port of Southampton as they prepared for an invasion of France. Scrope of Marsham discovered 'the Southampton Plot' which was being orchestrated by some of the King's closest and most trusted supporters. The plot was to unseat Henry as King. Scrope was loyal to the King and wanted to reveal all, but others had realised that he knew too much and pulled him behind a boat in the River Itchen -'the dark water'- so far that he could not have lived...

Southampton had been fortified against the French after they raided the town in 1338. 10,000 soldiers gathered there in 1415 and sailed to France where they were met by 30,000 French soldiers at Agincourt on 15 October 1415. The skilled Welsh bowmen with their long bows ensured an English victory and 11,000 French soldiers were killed on that day. Before he had left Southampton, Henry had heard of the plot against him and had had the conspirators captured and tried for treason.

Chrissie Stephen

6. A History of Cruise Ships

Southampton is one of three major ports within equidistance of London – the others being Dover and Harwich. There are four separate cruise terminals that are strung for two miles along the coast from west to east. The four terminals are: Mayflower, City, Ocean and Queen Elizabeth and only one cruise ship can be moored at each terminal. If an extra temporary terminal is needed, one can be used between Mayflower and City Terminal.

The first docks were created in 1843 and the first cruise ship that berthed was the P & O liner Ceylon. Southampton Docks has been owned by the British Port Authority since 1982 and today is the busiest cruise terminal and second largest container port. The average tidal range is 15.5 feet (4.7 metres) and for 17 hours each day there is rising water so this means that the cruise ships and container ship can access the port 80% of the time.

Most cruise ships arrive between 05:00-07:00. Most ships remain in the docks for the day and leave about 17.00. Records show that on average 1.2 million passengers arrive at Southampton - 300 cruise arrivals - which generates £1.25 million for the local economy. Southampton is the home port to P & O cruises, Celebrity Cruises, Cunard, Princess Cruises, Royal Caribbean and the ocean liner Queen Mary 2.

7. A Very Special Cruise Ship

With music and bunting and watched by a huge crowd, the world's most luxurious cruise liner, RMS Titanic, left Southampton on her maiden voyage on 10 April 1912. She was the largest ship afloat. Her first class accommodation was luxurious and she had many new safety features.

RMS Titanic sailed from Southampton to Cherbourg (France) and then to Queenstown (now Cobh in Ireland) and from there she sailed west towards the United States and the port of New York. Onboard were some of the world's wealthiest people and also a number of emigrants from Britain, Ireland and Scandinavia who were seeking a new life in the United States.

On the night of the 14 April, four days into her voyage and 600 km (375 miles) south of Newfoundland, RMS Titanic struck an iceberg. The ship's hull was buckled on the starboard side and five of the 16 watertight compartments were breached by the sea. There were only sufficient lifeboats for half of the ship's passengers. The ship sank within two hours and more than 1,500 passengers died that night.

The disaster shocked the world and there was outrage at the huge loss of life and this led to major improvements in maritime safety. Her wreck was found in 1985 and thousands of artifacts retrieved and put on display in museums around the world. RMS Titanic remains the second largest ocean liner wreck in the world. An informative display with an interactive model of the Titanic can be seen in the Sea City Museum.

8. Container Ships & Cargo

Southampton has the second largest deep sea container terminal in Britain (the largest is in Felixstowe) and was enlarged in 2013 so that it can handle the largest container ships in service.

The modern container terminal was built on reclaimed land and covers 210 acres, with a further 375 acres of storage available in the Old Port. The container port is always busy and can easily handle the loading and unloading of four large container ships simultaneously.

Following the enlargements, the terminal is now suitable for vessels up to 400 metres in length with a depth of up to 63 feet (19.2 metres).

The Port of Southampton can also handle the import and export of motor vehicles and has four multi-storey car parks for storage. The port handles four million tons of bulk goods each year including a huge amount of waste glass which is processed on site and made into cullet which is used to manufacture new glass.

The distinctive Rank Hovis flour mill processes 70,000 tons of wheat grain each year. There are refrigerator facilities for dealing with perishable foods and 82,000 tons of fresh fruit and vegetables are annually imported – mainly from the Canary Islands.

9. Famous People from Southampton & Waterside

There have been many famous people throughout history who have come from the area including Isaac Watts the Christian Minister and hymn writer who wrote more than 750 hymns that today are sung all over the world. Other historical figures include Sir Arthur Conan Doyle who wrote the Sherlock Holmes stories who lived in his later life in Minstead and is buried in the village churchyard.

Florence Nightingale is the most famous nurse of all time and she lived in Embley Park, Wellow where she died in 1910 and her grave can be seen in St Margaret's churchyard in East Wellow. Another famous lady who lived in the New Forest was Alice Pleasance Liddell who was the Alice in Lewis Carroll's famous stories.

Popular television naturalist Chris Packham was born in Southampton and now lives in the forest and is well known for his TV wildlife programmes, wildlife photography and children's books whilst another popular television personality was the comedian, Benny Hill (1924-1992).

Chrissie Stephen

Sir Ben Ainslie lives in Lymington and is four times sailing gold medalist in the Olympic Games (2000-2012) whilst Southampton snowboarder, Billy Morgan, won a bronze medal in the Winter Olympics in February 2018.

10. Serious Retail Therapy!

The great news is that Southampton in on the list of the UK's top ten shopping destinations! The city has two indoor shopping centres, a retail park, streets of small independent shops and a market which takes place every Friday and Saturday (09.00-17.00)

West Quay Shopping Centre is in a prestigious looking building that has 100 stores inside including many of the big names in retail. There are three floors of retail space with such popular stores as John Lewis and Marks & Spencer as well as iconic brands including Apple, Hollister and All Saints.

Because shopping can be hungry work, there is a complete food level called 'Dine at West Quay' with a great choice including handmade burgers, sushi, delicious pizzas and many other tasty options.

And if you haven't shopped enough...West Quay Retail Park is just a short distance away with a great selection of stores including Next, Boots, Furniture Village and Mama & Papas...

11. Eling Tide Mill

Eling Tide Mill is situated on the Forest side of the estuary (known locally as 'the Waterside') and is one of only two working tide mills in Britain (the other is Woolbridge Tide Mill in Suffolk).

The current mill has stood at Eling since 1785, but it is known that millers have been harnessing the power of the tides there for 900 years. The mill stands on Eling Creek, an artificial causeway and has a pair of independent water wheels that drive the mill stones which crush the wheat.

The mill is a Grade II listed building and recently there has been a great deal of conservation work completed on the mill and a new interactive exhibition centre and coffee shop have been created. It is interesting to see and a stroll along Eling Creek is fun, especially to see the local boys fishing for crabs with bacon tied on lines – a very successful way!

12. Hythe, With the Oldest Pier Railway

Hythe is a pretty market town on the Waterside that stands looking across Southampton Water to the town and its port. The view across from Hythe Marina is particularly good – especially if there is a cruise ship arriving or leaving.

Chrissie Stephen

The name Hythe means 'landing place' and there has been a settlement there for centuries and the name was first recorded in the 13th century. The Hythe Ferry has operated since the Middle Ages and was marked on local maps dated 1575 and 1788. Hythe has a small Victoria pier which was built in 1881 and measures 2,000 feet in length. It appears in the Guinness Book of Records as it has the oldest working pier train in the world – a two foot (576mm) gauge railway. In the early 20th century, there was an hourly steam boat crossing to Southampton and today there is still a regular ferry service

Hythe was the birthplace and home of the inventor of the hovercraft, Sir Christopher Cockerill, who worked in the town's ship building yard and ran the Hovercraft Development Company. The first successful hovercraft crossing was made on 25 July 1959 between Dover and Calais.

There is a really good weekly market in the town which is held on a Tuesday and Hythe is a pleasant place to wander especially as it has an attractive Georgian high street.

13. Dibden & Dibden Purlieu

The two villages of Dibden and Dibden Purlieu are both situated close to Hythe in the Waterside (on the eastern edge of the New Forest).

The village of Dibden Purlieu is first mentioned in the Doomsday Book (1086) but it was named 'Deepdene' – the Anglo Saxon word 'dene' meaning 'valley'. Its name changed in the 14th century when the boundaries of the New Forest were officially drawn up. As the village lay outside the new boundaries it was given the new name 'Deepdene Purlieu' – 'Purlieu' coming from the Norman French phrase meaning 'outskirts of the forest'.

The village of Dibden dates from the Middle Ages and it too gets its name from the Anglo Saxon word for valley as it lies in the valley which runs into Southampton Water. It has always been a rural community with farms but has been developed in the last 30 years as the power station at Fawley grew and new houses were needed by people working in Southampton. The village church of All Saints dates from 1291.

14. Fawley & the Oil Refinery

The ESSO refinery at Fawley certainly dominates the skyline on the Waterside. It is the largest refinery in the country and produces 22% of the country's capacity. The refinery's marine terminal stretches for one mile and handles 2,000 ships each year and about 25 million tons of crude oil.

Chrissie Stephen

The ESSO refinery is also the largest privately owned docks in Europe.

15. Calshot - With Such a Rich History

Calshot is situated at the western corner of Southampton Water where it joins the Solent. There is a pebbly spit which is a mile (3 km) in length and between it and the main coast there is an area of salty marshland which is popular with bird spotters.

Henry VIII recognised Calshot's importance in the defence of Southampton port so he had a castle built there in 1539.

Calshot became very important for the development of aircraft and later the flying boat and in 1913 RAF Calshot became established on the spit. Calshot continued to be a military garrison until 1956 and was a base for military flying boats. Calshot was also the first port radio and radar station.

The huge hangar used for the flying boats can still be seen today as it is now used as a popular activity centre for water sports (Calshot is perfect for wind surfing) and has a climbing and bouldering wall. There is also a velodrome for circuit cycling. Calshot also has a RNLI lifeboat service.

16. The Flying Boats

On 29 March 1913 Calshot Naval Air Station was opened by the Royal Flying Corps for testing the seaplanes and five years later it became a Royal Air Force Station with two flights of Felixstowe flying boats and sea planes. After the First World War, Calshot was used as the base for reconnaissance using the Felixstowe.

By the outbreak of the Second World War, there were still two operational squadrons at Calshot but they were relocated soon afterwards so that Calshot could be used mainly for repair and maintenance of short Sunderlands.

In May 1940, five sea planes from Calshot took part in the evacuation of Dunkirk and three aircraft carried more than 500 British troops back to safety and one of the aircraft made a successful second journey.

By 1946 and the end of the war, there were two squadrons based at Calshot, No 201 Sqn and No 230 Sqn - both with Sunderlands. The squadrons took part in the Berlin crisis in 1948, but shortly afterwards they were relocated to Pembroke and Calshot continued to be used as a marine craft and maintenance unit. For many years a sea plane was displayed near the hangar on the spit as a powerful reminder of Calshot's importance as a Royal Air Force base.

Chrissie Stephen

17. Calshot for Speed!

In the mid-1920s, it was decided that Calshot was perfect for high speed flight training for the Schneider Trophy Competition.

The competition took place in 1927 in Venice and the British team won which entitled them to host the competition at Calshot two years later in 1929. The S.5 aircraft covered the laps with an average speed of 328.62 mph and brought the trophy back to Britain for a second time. In 1931, the British team flying a Supermarine S6B won the competition for the third time.

As the teams practiced for the 1929 event, a young aircraftsman was posted to Calshot – Aircraftsman Law - who was none other than T.E Lawrence, better known as Lawrence of Arabia.

18. Pretty Coloured Beach Huts

One eye-catching feature at Calshot is the row of brightly painted beach huts that stand above the high water mark. Beach huts first appeared in 1862 and evolved from the Victorian bathing machines that had been designed to ensure modesty on the beach at all times!

After the Second World War, holidays in Britain became very fashionable and the first purpose built beach huts appeared either side of the pier in Bournemouth. Constructed in a similar way to a garden shed, beach huts became popular because they provided shelter from the sun and sea breezes and of course were perfect for modestly getting changed in and out of swimwear!

Beach huts were soon developed with the addition of simple cooking facilities – usually powered by camping gas – and were ideal for storing china, cutlery and comfortable beach chairs. Today there are still more than 21,000 beach huts in the UK – many of them privately owned and others rented. In recent years, a number of them have been sold at surprisingly high prices - similar to the cost of a flat in the area!

A few years ago, two new beach huts were built at Calshot and these were the first ones where people can stay overnight in them. They have been built to be environmentally friendly and despite their modest appearance, can sleep up to seven people.

19. The Isle of Wight

Just across the stretch of water known as 'The Solent' and just two miles (3.2 km) from Southampton, lies the Isle of Wight (IOW). The island has three distinctive large white chalk rocks that lie to its west and are known as 'The Needles' and sailors are protected from them by the 19th century lighthouse.

Chrissie Stephen

The island has been inhabited since the Neolithic Age and was first mentioned by Ptolemy. In the Iron Age when the sea level was lower, carts laden with tin were brought across to the island to be exported. Its geographical position means that it has always been used to defend the ports of Southampton and Portsmouth and was on the front line for Viking raids, the Spanish Armada and the Battle of Britain. It was inhabited by different tribes and communities and in Roman times was used as an agriculture area.

Since Victorian times it has been a popular holiday destination as it has a mild climate and 57 miles of coastline and tourism remains its main industry. The island has long had a boat building and sail making tradition and was also where flying boats and the hovercraft were developed – and Britain's space rockets.

20. Great Sailing...And A Good Rowing Challenge...

The Isle of Wight is an international sailing centre and Cowes Week is the longest running regatta in the world, attracting 1,000 yachts and 8,500 competitors with 50 different racing classics. Other sailing events include the Fastnet Race, Admiral's Cup and Commodore's Cup. The island is also listed as one of the top ten destinations for cyclists in the world and the Isle of Wight Randonnée is a popular annual cycling event.

There has also been a long tradition of rowing around the island, which is a distance of 60 miles (97km). The rowers must always row in an anti-clockwise direction around the island. In 1999 the first women successfully completed the circuit and the fastest men to date are Southampton rowers Chris Bennett and Roger Slaynake who set the record in 2003 of 8 hours 34 minutes.

21. A Royal Favourite

Victoria, the future Queen of England, spent much of her childhood on the Isle of Wight and it became her favourite holiday destination.

Her husband, Prince Albert, had Osborne House in East Cowes built for the Queen. Osborne House was built in an Italian style and soon became the Queen's favourite country house and she and Albert regularly spent time there with their nine children – especially through the winter months. Queen Victoria loved to walk and her favourite viewpoint called Egypt Point can still be visited today and lies between Cowes and Gurnard.

The Isle of Wight soon became fashionable with the Victorians as a holiday island and gaily coloured beach huts can still be seen at Appley, Seaview and Sandown. The poet Alfred, Lord Tennyson regularly visited the island as did Charles Dickens who wrote much of David Copperfield there. The island was a favourite destination for the French artist Morisot and members of European royalty

Chrissie Stephen

It was at Osborne House that the Queen died on 22 January 1901, aged 81 years old.

22. Dinosaur Island!

The Isle of Wight is the 'Dinosaur Capital' of Britain and one of the richest areas for fossils in Europe. Many fossils have been found on the island and even today, beaches Compton Beach and Yaverland are popular because it is still possible to find small ones there. There are organised walks with local experts and several dinosaur attractions on the island.

Dinosaur Isle is the first purpose-built museum dedicated just to dinosaurs and is situated by the sea wall in Sandown. The museum was built in the shape of a flying ptenosaur and inside, visitors step back 120 million years into a recreated dinosaur landscape with scale models of the other five dinosaurs that lived on the island – the Neovenator, Eotyrannus, Iguanodon, Hypsilophodon and Polacanthus.

At Blackgang Chine there is another attraction for 'dino lovers' called Restricted Area 5 and visited are warned that they enter at their peril as they will be greeted by a whole range of different life size moving dinosaurs!

23. The Importance of the Needles

The Needles have always been iconic to British travellers as once the three distinctive large chalk rocks are spotted at the western tip of the Isle of Wight, they know they are nearly home! Because of their position, the Needles have always been a defensive position.

It was at the Needle's Battery that the world's first radio was developed by Marconi in 1897. In 1898, the first paid telegram was sent from the battery and was called a Marconigram. Today, the National Wireless Museum at Ryde pays tribute to these important events.

The Needles Battery was also where the British space rockets Black Arrow and Black Knight were developed and on completion were transported to Australia for their launch.

24. Isle of Wight Crab Cakes

The Isle of Wight has always been known for its excellent fresh fruit and vegetables and fresh fish. The islanders have been farmers and fishermen since the Middle Ages. Of course crabs often get caught up in the fishing nets and this is a popular recipe on the island.

Chrissie Stephen

Ingredients:

- 750g cooked fresh crab meat
- 300g creamy mashed potato
- 1 medium beaten egg
- 4 spring onions – trimmed & chopped
- Good pinch of black pepper
- Good pinch of sea salt
- ½ tea cup of plain flour
- Olive oil for frying

Method:

In a large bowl combine all the ingredients except the flour and olive oil. Mix the mixture well. Cover the bowl with kitchen film and chill in the fridge for 30 minutes. Flour your hands well and divide the mixture into eight pieces and shape each into a fish cake about two inches (5 cm) in diameter. Dust each fish cake in turn and place on a plate. Heat the olive oil in a frying pan and fry the fish cakes gently for four minutes on each side. Serve straight away with a small jacket potato and a selection of green vegetables and some tartare sauce.

25. The Beautiful New Forest

The New Forest is situated west of Southampton Water and is one of the largest areas of open pasture land, heath land and forest in the UK. The New Forest covers southwest Hampshire, southeast Wiltshire and stretches towards East Dorset. The New Forest National Park is one of the newest National Parks in England. It was created in 2005 and extends to similar boundaries to the forest.

The New Forest covers 218 square miles (564 sq. km) with 89 sq. miles (230 sq. km) of woodland, 61 sq. miles (158 sq. km) of heath land, 57 sq. miles (147 sq. km) of farmland, 26 miles (42 km) of coastline and 141 miles (226 km) of footpaths.

The forest covers an area of 219 square miles (566 sq. km) and is drained by three rivers; the Lymington, Beaulieu and Avon. The highest point in the forest is Piper's Wait near Nomansland which is 432 feet (129 metres) above sea level.

With a rich history spanning a thousand years, there are a number of amusing old English names to be found in the area including Little Stubby Hat, Antony's Bee Bottom and Sandy Balls!

Chrissie Stephen

26. A Rich History

There has been a forest in the area since Roman times, but following the Norman Conquest in 1066, it was declared a Royal Forest by William 1 (the Conqueror) who loved to hunt for deer. In the Doomsday Book (1078) it is referred to as Nova Foresta and interestingly, was the only forest to be described in great detail.

William the Conqueror was a frequent visitor to the forest to take part in hunting parties and two of his sons were killed in the forest. Prince Richard died in 1081 and the king's second son, William Rufus was mortally wounded by an arrow in 1100. The Rufus Stone (in Minstead near Lyndhurst) marks the spot where the price fell.

Local folklore told how the king had been punished by God for creating the New Forest because in doing so he had destroyed 20 hamlets and farmsteads.

By 1698 the area of the New Forest had been confined by statute and within a few years, the Royal Navy was using it as a source of timber for ships and new plantations of trees were planted for this purpose. During the First World War (1914-1918) broad leaved trees were felled for timber that was needed for the war and were replaced by conifers. The same thing happened during the Second World War (1939-1945), but this time, the process was reversed with some plantations being returned to heath land. Even today, 90% of the New Forest is owned by the Crown and it is managed by the Verderers, supported by Forest Law.

>TOURIST

27. Ponies Galore!

A common sight in the forest is the beautiful New Forest pony. There have been ponies in the area since 500 BC and they are one of the native moorland pony breeds of Britain and their breeding is strictly controlled. The ponies are 12-14 hands and usually grey, bay or chestnut in colour. This breed is known to be strong and hardy and also good for riding.

If you are visiting the New Forest in the spring or summer you may well see mares and their foals as they are free to roam. Many of the foals will be sold at the special sales in Beaulieu Road.

A register of stallions is held by the Verderers who decide which ones will be let out to breed between April-July. They choose the stallions careful so that the breed is preserved and each stallion will only breed for 3- 4 seasons. There are five Agisters who work for the Verderers and they are each allocated an area and are responsible for the ponies in it and it is they who will attend any accident involving one of 'their' ponies.

Once a year they gather the ponies in drifts (groups) to give them a health check, to de-worm them and to mark them. Each of the ponies is owned by a 'commoner' – local people who have 'rights of common pasture'. Their pony will be branded so that it can be recognised and if the marking fees have been paid, the Agister will cut the pony's tail in his own distinct pattern.

39

Although the ponies look friendly, they are wild and a local bye law prohibits the public from feeding them – anyone found doing so will be fined £200.

28. Nature's Treasure Trove

The forest has a number of important habitats including valley bogs, wet heath lands and deciduous woodland and these support a rich number of wild flowers, insects and mammals. More than 700 different types of wild flowers grow in the New Forrest - 32% of the total number that grow in Britain and 2,700 different fungi. There are deer, newts and several species of bats.

A number of rare species of wildlife can also be found. The most unusual of these is the New Forest Cicada (Cicadetta montana) which is the only cicada that is native to Britain but unfortunately, it has not been recorded in the forest for more than ten years.

Rare plants thrive in the area, the most unusual being the wild gladiolus (Gladolus illynous). There are a number of rare insects that thrive in the natural environment of the New Forest including the Southern Damselfly (Coenagrian mercuriale) and mole cricket (Gryllotaipa gryllotaipa) and among reptiles, the sand lizard Laceta agilis). Needless to say, the New Forest is deemed a Site of Scientific Interest (SSSI), Special Area of Conservation (SAC), Special Protection Area for Birds (SPA) and is also a RAMSAR site. The New Forest is currently being considered as a future World Heritage Site by UNESCO.

29. Pannage

The tradition of Pannage still continues in the New Forest. Pannage is the releasing of domestic pigs in the forest to eat acorns and other nuts which are poisonous for other animals such as ponies and cows if eaten in any quantity.

Pannage lasts for a 60 day period and has a variable starting date each year as it is determined by the acorns starting to fall from the trees. Owners must not allow their pigs to feed in the forest at any other times of the year except if they have pregnant sows – known as 'privileged sows' as they can feed at any time!

Pannage used to be common throughout Britain but today it only takes place in the New Forest. In the Doomsday Book land was measured by Pannage – 'wood for the pannage of forty hogs'.

The New Forest has had a long tradition of hunting and has many local recipes that have used game from the forest. This recipe uses pheasant and Chanterelle mushrooms that grow in a few locations there. It is cooked slowly in a range or slow cooker so that the flavours really develop.

Ingredients:

- 1 pheasant (about 1.5 kg /3lb in weight)
- 8 oz. /200g streaky bacon – chopped
- 1 large onion – peeled and chopped

Chrissie Stephen

- 450g (1lb) Chanterelle mushrooms – chopped
- 600ml (1 pint) dry white wine
- 150 ml (¼ pint) chicken stock
- 2 bay leaves
- 1 tablespoon each fresh chopped thyme and rosemary
- 2 tablespoons of butter

Method:

Preheat the slow cooker. In a large frying and melt the butter. Rub the pheasant generously with salt and pepper and then cook in the butter until browned all over. Transfer meat to the slow cooker. In the pan add the onions and mushrooms, cook gently for 5 minutes. Add the wine and stock simmer for 10 minutes. Add the herbs and then pour mixture into the slow cooker. Cover and cook on low for seven hours – turning the pheasant regularly. Serve sprinkled with fresh parsley.

31. Beaulieu

Beaulieu is a pretty small village that is situated on the southeastern edge of the New Forest. Its name comes from the French meaning 'beautiful place'. Today, it is one of the most popular tourist attractions in southern England as it is home to the British National Motor Museum. The village has more than 900 years of heritage.

>TOURIST

There was once a Royal hunting lodge in Beaulieu for when the king came to the New Forest to hunt. In 1204 King John gave the land as a gift to the Cistercian monks who built an abbey there. The community flourished until the 1530s when Henry VIII began his dissolution of the monasteries as part of his schism from the Roman Catholic Church. Beaulieu was sold to one of the King's friends – the First Earl of Southampton in 1538 for the sum of £1,340 6s 8d. Over the years, few of its owners ever lived in the lodge until 1867 when Lord Henry Scott moved into the village and transformed Palace House into his home.

In 1952 Edward, Lord Montagu opened Palace House and its gardens to the public – making it one of the first stately homes to be opened.

32. Palace House

Palace House is a beautiful looking building that stands overlooking the picturesque Beaulieu River millpond.

In the 13th century Palace House was built as the main gate house to the abbey. The abbey and its grounds (it was an 8,000 estate) were sold to the First Earl of Southampton in 1538, who did live in the gate house, but it remained untouched until the late 19th century when Lord Henry Scott began to live there permanently. Palace house was completely renovated and was transformed into a fine Victoria country house.

Chrissie Stephen

The house is open to the public and is regarded as one of the finest stately homes and because it has been a family home it has a homely character. In fact, visitors were often surprised and delighted to hear music coming from the library as Edward, Lord Montagu relaxed reading the paper! Access to the library is interesting as it is through a concealed entrance, through a door that looks just like a bookshelf!

In the last few years, the kitchens have been renovated and restored back to their original layout and it is not unusual to find the family cook at work!

* The oldest piece of furniture in Palace House is the Abbot's Bread Cupboard – a small rectangular cupboard made from carved oak and dating from the 14th century.

33. Beaulieu Abbey

Beaulieu Abbey was founded between 1203-1284 By King John who brought 30 Cistercian monks from the Order's main abbey in Citreaux, France. They named the abbey Bellus Loucus Regis – beautiful palace of the king - and over the years this changed to the modern name, Beaulieu.

The abbey was sizeable and took 40 years to complete. The abbey was 102 metres long with a semi-circular apse and 11 radiating chapels. Work was completed in 1246. There was a refectory, kitchens, sleeping quarters and an infirmary, and out buildings too including workshops and stables.

The first Abbot of the Abbey was Hugh, who found great favour with the King and was often sent on diplomatic missions. He was greatly rewarded for his efforts by the king who gave him land in the New Forest, cattle, wine and money and was eventually made Bishop of Carlisle. When Henry III came to the throne, he too highly favoured the abbey and gave them gifts and soon the abbey was very rich.

The abbey was closed under Henry V III's dissolution of the monasteries and was bought by Thomas Wriothesley, First Earl of Southampton, who never lived there as he preferred the main gate building which today is Palace House. Some of the abbey still remains and today the refectory is the church. The abbey is said to be one of the most haunted places in Britain and many have seen monks dressed in brown or white and heard strange Gregorian chants.

34. A Passion for Cars...

When Palace House was opened to the public in 1952 there was a grand opening and for it Edward, Lord Montagu put five veteran cars on display in the entrance hall as a tribute to his father, John Douglas-Scott-Montagu, who had been a motoring pioneer at the turn of the 20th century. Lord Montagu was surprised and delighted by the interest in the cars and encouraged by the growing public interest in motoring heritage, the Montagu Motoring Museum was founded.

Chrissie Stephen

Lord Montagu received a great deal of support from motoring enthusiasts and the motor trade and soon the collection of cars began to grow and the cars were displayed in a series of wooden sheds. By 1964, the museum was being visited by half a million people and it was time to construct a new museum building

By 1972, the museum had 300 exhibits and had outgrown its building so a new larger one was built. In the same year, it became the National Motor Museum – an independent charitable trust – and this change coincided with the launch of the Jaguar XJ12 – truly a time of celebration for the British motor industry.

Today visitors enjoy the selection of exhibits that include some late 19th century vehicles and some popular on screen motors including Rodney's Reliant Royal from television's Only Fools & Horses and Mr Bean's famous lime green Mini!

35. And for Chocolates!

Beaulieu High Street is very pretty and just a short distance from the Mill Pond. There are a number of attractive shops for browsing and one that's definitely for eating!

Beaulieu Chocolate Studio is at No 1 High Street and has an irresistible selection of beautiful homemade chocolates in its window. Beaulieu has had a tradition for chocolate making since the 1980s. The original shop closed in 2006 and was relocated in the current building which was once the village Patisserie. There are two parts to the chocolate studio; the workshop and the retail section and it is possible to stay awhile and watch the chocolates being made.

Trevor the owner, trained as a baker and chocolatier in France and once owned a shop in the Loire. Today the Beaulieu Chocolate Studio makes a selection of 30 different filled chocolates as well as gift boxes and seasonal specials including Easter bunnies. The most popular chocolate of them all is the New Forest Bark and the box of six chocolates shaped as motor cars...

36. Hatchet Pond

Hatchet Pond is the largest pond in the New Forest and is situated just one mile west of Beaulieu. The pond was artificially created in the 18th century to provide power for the local iron mill. The mill has long since gone but the pond has remained as is really valuable for its natural habitat.

Amongst its natural treasures, the pond has three of all the wetland plants found in the UK and 100 different species of freshwater insects. The pond is popular with course fishermen too as it has good stocks of roach, tench, bream and carp. Hatchet Pond is popular with walkers as there is a pleasant circular walk around the pond which is two miles (3km) in length.

Chrissie Stephen

37. Bucklers Hard

Situated on the banks of the Beaulieu river stands the pretty hamlet of Buckler's Hard. Today the attractive avenue of Georgian cottages leads down to the waters front and the yacht marina. Its small museum reveals the hamlet's past importance. Buckler's Hard is part of the Beaulieu Estate and is situated 2.5 miles (4km) from Beaulieu. It was created by the Second Duke of Montagu as a free port for trade with the West Indies, but soon began shipbuilding as there was a good supply of timber for the hulls from the nearby New Forest.

Ship building began in the early 18th century when the ship yard was run by James Wyatt from Hythe who won a contract to build two ships for the Navy – HMS Surprise and HMS Scorpion in 1744. Over the next 60 years, the ship yard was to build a total of 43 ships including several for Nelson's navy and these took part in the Battle of Trafalgar in 1805. For the next 100 years or more, ship building declined, but during the Second World War, Bucklers Hard became important for producing torpedo boats. Buckler's Hard was also the gathering point for hundreds of vessels involved in the allied operation of the Normandy landings – Operation Overlord – which began on 6 June 1944.

Today there is a small maritime museum there that traces the importance of the ship yard with some interesting artifacts including Nelson's baby clothes and a lock of his hair! One of the Georgian houses is called 'Ship Builder's Cottage' and is open to the public and a church is situated in another of the houses and a good pub in a third!

38. The Jewel of the New Forest

Exbury Gardens sit in 200 acres of land near the village of Exbury, just east of Beaulieu and across the Beaulieu river from Bucklers Hard. The informally styled gardens were built in 1919 by Lionel Nathan de Rothschild, close to his family home in the village. Today, the gardens are world famous for their stunning displays of rhododendrons, azaleas and camellias. There is the riverside walk to enjoy, the hydrangea walk, the rock gardens and the sundial garden. Exbury Gardens can be explored on foot, by chauffeur driven buggy or aboard the popular steam railway (12 ¼" / 311 mm gauge).

The gardens are open for most of the year and are glorious when they are full of springtime tulips and daffodils or the rich colours of autumn. Many visitors enjoy seeing the stunning 'Azalea Bowl' during the month of May. Perfect for relaxing, there are tea rooms at Exbury, frequent painting exhibitions and various children's activities.

39. Lepe Country Park

Lepe is situated within the New Forest and the Country Park runs for one mile (3 km) from Stanswood Bay eastwards to the mouth of the Beaulieu River. Part of the Country Park is on the shore of the Solent and has great views of the Isle of Wight – needless to say it becomes a popular place with spectators during Cowes Week! There

Chrissie Stephen

are two parts to Lepe; the clifftop area with its grassy meadow and the beach. There is the five mile (8km) long circular walk called the 'Lepe Loop'.

In Roman times, Lepe was a harbour and in the 18th century it was being used for shipbuilding but by 1825 was completely silted up. It continued to be used as a look out point by coastguards – which it still is today Lepe was also used for many years for the local oyster trade. It was hidden during the Second World War and used for constructing huge concrete caissons (Phoenix breakwaters) which were towed across the English Channel to be used for the artificial Mulberry Harbour after D Day. Lepe was also the site on the mainland for PLUTO (Pipe-Lines Under The Ocean) which carried fuel to the Isle of Wight and then on to the Allied Forces in Normandy.

The shingle beach is not recommended for swimming, but it is a great vantage point for watching boats in the Solent. It is a popular spot for bird watchers as the mud flats attract Brent Geese, Curlews, Oyster Catchers, Dunlin and Plover. The fresh water ponds on the edge of the Country Park attract Redshanks, Herons and Kingfishers – amongst others!

40. Oysters by the Ton!

Since Roman times, the Solent has been an important area for oysters and was once the most important oyster fishery in Europe. At the peak of production in the 1920s, 40 million oysters were processed.

The industry began to diminish due to over-fishing, habitat loss and disease. By the 1960s just three million were being produced but stocks were strengthened by imported young oysters and in 1974 there were 450 vessels and 700 local fishermen working in the industry, producing 15 million oysters. In the following years the industry began to falter once again and by 2007 just 200 tonnes of oysters were caught and 20 tonnes in 2011 – which is about 250,000 oysters. Things grew so bad that in 2013 oyster fishing was banned in the Solent.

A special five year project was launched last autumn in the area to try and revive the industry. The project is being run by Blue Marine Foundation in conjunction with marine biologists at Portsmouth University. One million young oysters have been put in the Solent between Southampton and the Isle of White in an attempt to revive stocks and a further 10,000 young oysters have been placed in special marine cages located in several local harbours. The re-establishment of the oyster beds will have a positive impact as they support other marine life too and every single oyster filters 200 litres of sea water – an effective way to clean up the sea providing there are no negative effects on the oysters!

Chrissie Stephen

41. Lymington

The pretty market of Lymington lies on the west bank of the Lymington river overlooking the Solent. It is a historic town that was an Iron Age hill fort and later an Anglo Saxon village and sea port. Lymington is referred to as Lentune in the Doomsday Book.

From the Middle Ages until the 19th century, Lymington was famous for its production of sea salt. In 1346 the town produced war ships for Edward III and it did so again in the 16th century for Henry VIII. Ship building continued in the town until the 19th century.

The original part of the town is the pretty cobbled streets with their Georgian and Victorian buildings. The main street leads down to the quayside where luxury yachts mingle with the fishing boats. Local stories tell of smugglers and of hidden passages under the cobbled streets. Today, Lymington is a major yachting centre with three marinas.

Saturday is market day and the stalls stretch up the hill on either side of the main street. There are fruit and vegetable stalls and others selling crafts and antiques. Lymington is the perfect place for browsing as it has some lovely shops – especially in the Old Town and there is the chance to enjoy traditional English afternoon tea in one of the old fashioned tea shops.

42. The Story of the Golden Post Box

Sir Ben Ainslie CBE is an English competitive sailor competing in both Laser and Finn dinghy competitions. He is the most successful sailor in Olympic history...and he lives in Lymington.

He has won five medals in five different Olympic Games since 1996 when he won a silver medal when he was just 19 years old. Has won four gold medals between 2000-2012, and on 19 May 2012 he became the first person to carry the Olympic torch on British soil and following his success at the London Olympics that year the town decided to honour him by painting the main post box in the centre of the town, gold.

Ben Ainslie remains a member of the Royal Lymington Yacht Club. HM Queen has given him three honours - an MBE, CBE and a knighthood.

Chrissie Stephen

43. Rhinefield – a Great Ornamental Drive

Situated not far from Brockenhurst, Rhinefield is a delightful ornamental drive that can be enjoyed on foot or bike too. The main car park is at Blackwater and from there, two walks can be enjoyed. The first is the shorter walk and visits the arboretum and the second is the Tall Trees Walk.

The Tall Trees Walk is great to do in May/June time because as well as the wonderful smell of fresh pine, there are lofty Redwood and Douglas Fir trees to admire and plenty of rhododendron, which are in full flower in late spring. The Douglas Firs are the oldest in Britain and were planted in 1859 when 'exotic trees' were fashionable.

There is a sensory trail too which encourages everyone to use all their senses – particularly smell and touch. The Arboretum features trees from all over the world and leads on to the Bolderwood ornamental drive.

The Rhinefield Drive walk is a circular route beginning and ending at the car park and passes the beautiful Rhinefield House Hotel which is a grand country house dating from 1887 – and the perfect place to enjoy afternoon tea!

>TOURIST

44. Brockenhurst

This delightful village has a great deal to live up to as it has been voted the UK's most beautiful village. Surrounded by the New Forest there is the chance to see ponies, cattle and deer. Brockenhurst is the largest village in the Forest. The first settlement there was in the Bronze Age. During the Saxon period, there were four manor houses and the fourth, Brocaste was the largest and most important and gave the village its name.

During the First World War the Lady Hardinge Hospital for Wounded Soldiers in the village, cared for soldiers whom had been injured in India and this is why several of the roads in the village have Indian names. During the Second World War, the Balmer Lawn Hotel was the secret meeting place for General Montgomery and President Eisenhower as they plotted the D Day landings.

Today, there are several beautiful hotels and good restaurants in the village including The Pig which is both!

The Weir stream flows through the village and joins the Lymington River. At one place it crosses the Brookley Road at a point known by locals as 'The Splash'. A little further on there is a river beach known as 'Brock Beach' which is popular with families when the water is warm enough for paddling!

Chrissie Stephen

45. New Forest Wildlife Park

Situated close to the village of Ashurst, this is a fascinating place to visit as there is the chance to see various species that are or were native to the UK in their natural surroundings. There are red deer, fallow deer, several species of otters and wild boar. There is an established badger sett with a labyrinth of entrances and exits to the sett and it is not unusual for these to number 25-30. There are 15 different species of owl to see too and some impressive wolves.

There is a large tropical butterfly house which is housed in a huge glasshouse filled with a wide variety of tropical plants and flowers and it is open from springtime through to the autumn so visitors can walk through at their own pace admiring the myriad of different species.

An important aspect of the Park's work is conservation and also the rehabilitation of sick or injured owls, deer, otter and foxes.

There are themed and seasonal trails to enjoy at the Wildlife Park and a variety of talks through the day. There are various feeding times to attend – with the otters being the most entertaining of all!

>TOURIST

46. Lyndhurst

The bustling town of Lyndhurst is the administrative centre of the New Forest and in the impressive Queen's House, the ancient Court of the Verderers meets regularly to discuss all aspects of the administration and enforcement of by-laws in the New Forest.

The town is mentioned in the Doomsday Book (1086) with the name 'Linhest' but its name evolved into Lyndhurst – Lynd meaning 'lime tree' and 'hurst' - 'wooded hill'.

There is a popular local story that mentions the slaying of a dragon on the outskirts of the town. The dragon was said to live at Burley Beacon and was terrorising everyone. A young knight called Berkley was able to slay the dragon at Bolton's Bench and peace was restored! The churchyard of St Michael & All Angels is visited by many to see the grave of Alice Liddell – the inspiration for Alice in Wonderland by Lewis Carroll.

Today the town has a collection of different shops and restaurants as well as places to stay. The place where many like to go 'window shopping' is the car showroom at the bottom end of the High Street as there are numerous gleaming Ferrari and Maserati on display!

The New Forest Centre is interesting as it details the history of the forest and its wildlife, with information about the conservation of this beautiful National Park.

Chrissie Stephen

47. Romsey

Although not strictly in The Waterside, Romsey is a popular place to visit for cruise passengers as it is quintessentially English. Romsey (pronounced Rumsey) is situated just seven miles (11 km) northwest of Southampton and is the main town on the River Test.

This delightful market town was home to the 19th century Prime Minister, Lord Palmerston and later, Louis Mountbatten, 1st Earl of Burma. The town's name comes from 'Rum's Eg' meaning 'Rum's area by the marsh'. The first abbey was built in AD 907 by King Edward the Elder for his daughter Princess Aethelflaed who was a nun. Romsey became a strong religious community. The present Romsey Abbey dates from the Norman period and by 1240 was home to 100 nuns. In 1348 the Black Death killed half of the nuns and prosperity never returned to the abbey.

In the Middle Ages, it became important in the woollen industry for dying and weaving wool before it was exported from Southampton. By the mid-18th century, competition from the northern mills was too strong and attention was turned to two new industries – paper making and sack making which both used water from the River Test.

When Lord Palmerston was Prime Minister he lived at Broadlands on the edge on the town and later, this was home to Lord Mountbatten. Embley Park on the edge of the town, was home to Florence Nightingale. She is said to have had her calling from God whilst sitting under a giant cedar tree there.

48. Lord Mountbatten

Prince Louis of Battenberg was born on 25 June 1900 in Windsor and was a cousin of Prince Philip and second cousin twice removed of HM Queen Elizabeth II. In 1917, his family stopped using their German names and he became Louis Mountbatten. He was a British naval officer and statesman. During the Second World War he was the Supreme Allied Commander Southeast Asia Command (1943-46). It was he who received the receipt of the Japanese surrender. Lord Mountbatten was the last Viceroy of India and first Governor- General of independent India.

In 1947 he was given the earldom and also a second title of Baron Romsey of Romsey. H.M the Queen and Prince Philip spent their honeymoon at Broadlands after their wedding in 1947 and HRH Prince Charles and Diana, Princess of Wales did the same following their wedding in 1981.

Lord Mountbatten, his grandson Nicholas, and two other people were killed by an IRA bomb that blew up their fishing boat in County Sligo in Ireland in August 1979. After a ceremonial funeral at Westminster Abbey, Lord Mountbatten was laid to rest in his beloved Romsey Abbey.

Chrissie Stephen

49. The City of the Statues

Like Romsey, the beautiful city of Winchester is a popular destination for visitors to Southampton. There has been a settlement there since prehistoric times and in the Iron Age it was a cluster of three hill forts. During Roman times, Winchester was known as Venta Belgarum and in the 3rd century was the largest and most important town in England.

The first church was built in the 7th century and a new cathedral was built on the same spot in 1079. Winchester Cathedral is one of the largest cathedrals in Europe and has the longest Gothic nave. The grave of the novelist Jane Austen can be seen in the cathedral. Winchester became an important place of pilgrimage. During the Middle Ages and its name was changed to the Old English name Winton-Ceastre.

A walk along the High Street reveals a variety of architectural styles and the famous 15th century Buttercross which has 12 statues including the Virgin Mary, saints and historical figures. There are three other statues to see in the vicinity. The statue of Queen Victoria was carved by Sir Alfred Gilbert who is famous for his statue of Eros in Piccadilly Circus. Facing the city there is an impressive statue of King Alfred with his raised sword and the third statue is entitled Horse & Rider at the entrance to the courts. Winchester is a university town and has the oldest public school to still be situated in its original buildings. For those who want to browse around the shops, there is a good selection with traditional coffee shops and tea rooms too.

50. Knights and Bollards!

Another popular place to visit in Winchester is the castle with its Great Hall of the old castle. The Great Hall was built in 1235 and is famous for King Arthur's Round Table which has hung on its wall since the 15th century. During the Middle Ages, festivals called Round Tables were held throughout Europe with jousting, dancing and feasting.

The table was originally unpainted but Henry VIII had it painted in 1522 – probably for a Round Table festival. King Arthur is depicted sitting on his throne at the head of the table and around the edge of the table are the names of all his legendary knights – but on closer inspection, 'King Arthur' can be seen to be Henry VIII! Near the Great Hall are Queen Eleanor's Gardens which are filled with the plants and perfumes that were commonly grown in 13th century England.

Walking between Great Minister Street and The Square, there is a collection of 24 eye-catching traffic bollards that have been hand painted in the styles of famous artists. Amongst the collection there is a bollard painted in the style of Henri Matisse 'Beast of the Sea', another in the style of Gustav Klimt's 'Fulfilment' and a third is dedicated to Pablo Picasso's Le Rêve (The Dream). The most popular bollard of all, is the one dedicated to the Mona Lisa by Leonardo da Vinci.

Chrissie Stephen

TOP REASONS TO BOOK THIS TRIP

If you are visiting Southampton whilst on a cruise, you will have the opportunity to enjoy an excursion to some of the places mentioned in this guide...

Places of Interest: Something of interest for all the family.

Quintessentially English: The chance to enjoy traditional English Countryside, food and shopping.

Historical Interest: Places with a rich heritage from Medieval Times.

> TOURIST
GREATER THAN A TOURIST

Visit GreaterThanATourist.com:
http://GreaterThanATourist.com

Sign up for the Greater Than a Tourist Newsletter:
http://eepurl.com/cxspyf

Follow us on Facebook:
https://www.facebook.com/GreaterThanATourist

Follow us on Pinterest:
http://pinterest.com/GreaterThanATourist

Follow us on Instagram:
http://Instagram.com/GreaterThanATourist

Follow on Twitter:
http://twitter.com/ThanaTourist

Chrissie Stephen

> TOURIST
GREATER THAN A TOURIST

Please leave your honest review of this book on Amazon and Goodreads. Thank you. We appreciate your positive and constructive feedback. Thank you.

Chrissie Stephen

NOTES

Printed in Great Britain
by Amazon